CONGRATULATIONS!

YOU'RE NOT PREGNANT

CONGRATULATIONS!
YOU'RE NOT PREGNANT

An illustrated guide to birth control   by Peter Mayle & Arthur Robins

Macmillan Publishing Co.Inc. New York

Designed by Maggie Lewis

Library of Congress cataloging number 81–4829.

Macmillan Publishing Co. Inc.
866 Third Avenue, New York, N.Y. 10022,
Collier Macmillan Canada, Ltd.

10 9 8 7 6 5 4 3 2 1

Printed in Hong Kong

INTRODUCING HIS AND HERS

It seems amazing in these enlightened times, but it's true: every year, millions of babies are conceived by accident.

In the United States alone during 1978, over 500,000 teenage girls became mothers. For the vast majority of them, pregnancy came as an unpleasant surprise.

Why does it happen? Not because of a lack of contraceptives; they're more plentiful and easier to get now than they've ever been, providing you know where to go and what to ask for. But that's the problem. When you're young, you *don't* always know where to go and what to ask for. And good advice is sometimes difficult to find.

You're embarrassed to ask your parents, and they're embarrassed even to bring the subject up, let alone go into the details of pills, condoms, diaphragms, caps, spermicidal jellies and the rhythm method – the whole business is enough to make them choke on their cornflakes.

We hope this book will help. It won't give you any moral guidance on whether you should or shouldn't make love in the first place. That's a personal decision you have to make for yourself.

Nor is it supposed to be a medical textbook. But it does give you the basic facts about conception and contraception, and a review of the most popular methods of birth control. If, after reading about them you still decide to cross your fingers and hope for the best, that's up to you. But at least you'll know a bit more about the chances you're taking.

The two main characters in the chapters that follow are you and your partner. Or, to put it another way, the penis and the vagina.

There they are, a handsome pair, on the opposite page.

There are probably more myths and misunderstandings about these two friendly parts of the anatomy than about any other parts of our bodies. They fascinate us from babyhood onwards. And, from time to time, we worry about them. These worries, which feel very personal and new, have in fact been with us for thousands of years, rather like standard equipment we're issued with as we grow up.

Practically everybody we know has had them. Practically nobody admits to them at the time.

SIZE

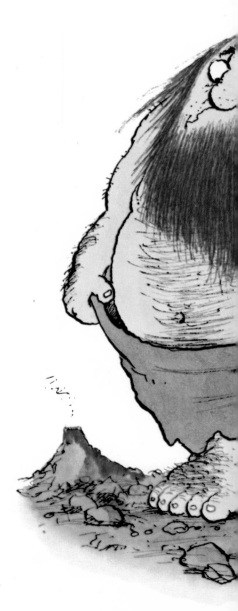

Ever since man first looked downwards, he has shown a lifelong interest in the size of his penis, and a sneaking interest in the size of everybody else's. The same applies, though to a lesser extent, to woman and her vagina. The fact is that most men and most women are created roughly equal in terms of size.

Occasional monsters and midgets do crop up in both sexes, but any significant difference from the average is rare.

The average penis is about six inches long when standing to attention. In the at ease position, sizes can vary considerably. And since that's when you're most likely to see other men's penises, that's probably where the myth about big differences in size gets started. The smaller a penis is when at rest, the more it grows in the process of erection. The larger it is to start with, the less it grows. The end result is about the same.

The vagina isn't as easy to measure, partly because it's inside, and partly because it's a passage capable of almost miraculous elasticity. If you're worried that your vagina is too small, don't be. A vagina can expand to allow the exit of a baby,

so it can certainly handle the entry of a penis. The only times you'll have difficulty are when the entrance is blocked by the hymen (which we describe later), or when the muscles in your vagina are tensed up and unyielding.

Fortunately, it's very unusual for a vagina to be too large, either. Even if yours is on the generous side, you can still achieve just as much sexual enjoyment for both of you by experimenting with your positions when you make love.

Another important thing for both of you to remember is that size in itself, without skill, is no guarantee of sexual happiness. It's no more useful than an eight-foot basketball player who can't find the basket.

PERFORMANCE

We seem to be surrounded by couples who enjoy terrific sex lives. We see them in films, we read about them in books, and we watch them on TV commercials nibbling chocolate bars and deodorizing their armpits as a prelude to sexual bliss. All this highly romanticized propaganda conditions us to expect sexual perfection from the word go. And if our own first efforts don't measure up, we're disappointed, discouraged, and maybe even feel that there's something wrong with us.

There's nothing wrong at all, except that real life is never quite as well-arranged as fiction. You wouldn't expect to jump into a car and be able to drive without having had some practice. And you can't expect to jump into bed and become a sexual star overnight.

Unfortunately, most of us would rather admit to having bad breath than being disappointed or disappointing in bed. We're all guilty of encouraging the myth of perfection. Who likes to admit to being a flop?

And yet we all start as amateurs, and we all have sexual off days.

It helps to admit that, even if only to yourself, and to try to relax about it. The less you and your partner worry about your own problems, the more fun both of you will have. Easier said than done, but true just the same.

WORKING PARTS

When you first think about it, you may wonder how the penis and the vagina can ever get up to anything. The penis is droopy. The vagina seems impossibly small. What happens to them before that delightful moment when one slips into the other?

In the case of the penis, the process starts when your brain sends down a message as a result of something or someone you've seen or touched or thought about. This message causes an extra supply of blood to come rushing into your penis from other parts of your body. The blood pumps up the penis to make it bigger, stiffer, and prepared for action. The sperm, who have been lurking in a sac near your testicles waiting for just such an opportunity, are eager to escape through the hole at the end of your penis. You're all set; and there, on the brink of great excitement, we'll leave you while we see what's happening to the vagina.

Similar and wonderful events have been taking place here as well. Again, the brain has sent down the good news, and blood has been diverted to your vagina. You then begin to produce a colourless, slippery fluid which lubricates the entrance to your vagina and the passage itself. The lips of your vagina, and the clitoris just above them, become more sensitive and prominent. Now you're ready as well. The time has come for the penis to enter the vagina.

In a perfect world, the penis and the vagina reach the point of all systems go at about the same time. Much more often, though, the penis reaches orgasm before the vagina, and many a man has come and gone before the woman is really ready. This is a letdown for both of you, particularly the woman, but patience and experience will help you get your timing right.

In fact, the foreplay leading up to the penis entering the vagina is one of the best parts of making love. Anything goes, providing you both enjoy it: kissing and nibbling, licking and sucking, stroking and squeezing. Although the area round the genitals is obviously the most sensitive spot for both of you (particularly the clitoris for the woman), don't forget the rest of your bodies. Ears, neck, nipples, buttock, armpits, toes—almost every part of your body has nerve endings which respond to the right treatment.

It's impossible to generalize too much about such a personal act. The main thing to remember is that the more time you spend on foreplay, the more satisfying final intercourse is likely to be for both of you. You may not get it right first go, but you'll have a wonderful time practising.

THE SPERM AND THE EGG: A TRUE ROMANCE

There's nothing mysterious about birth control. But you'll find it easier to understand if you have a working knowledge of exactly how the process of birth starts in the first place.

A baby begins when the male sperm meet the female egg, and fertilize it.

Not just one sperm, but millions of them, are produced continuously by the male hormones and are stored in the sac near your testicles waiting for their big moment. Their sole ambition in life is to get out and do a bit of fertilizing, but they need the co-operation of your penis before they can get to work. Although a few sperm can leak out of a resting penis, a mass escape can only take place when the penis is erect. You've probably had erections at all sorts of time when you were least expecting them. That's one indication of how keen the sperm are to leave home.

The actual moment when the sperm leave the penis, called ejaculating or coming, usually happens as a result of friction that takes place between the penis and the vagina (or a hand). We say usually, because it sometimes happens without

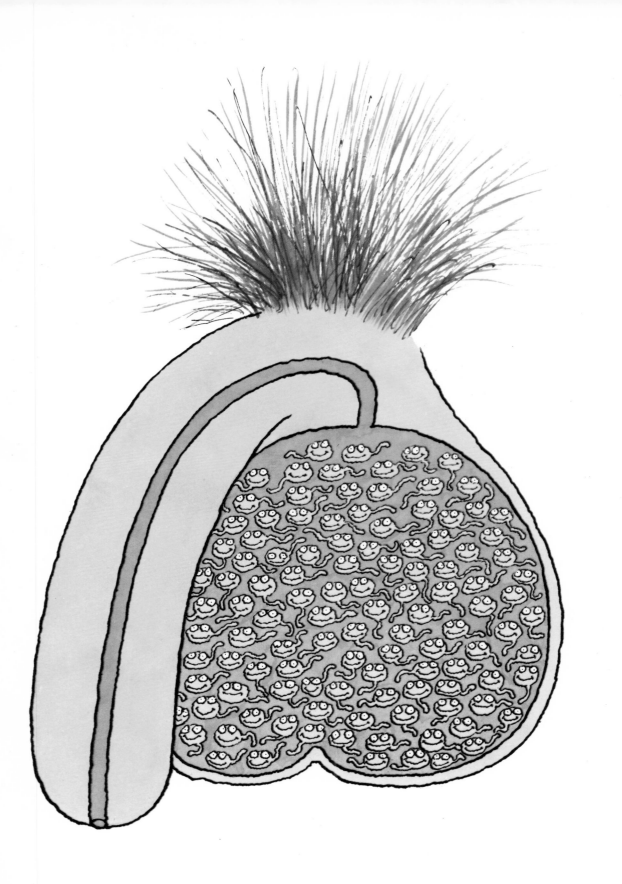

any outside help at all. Wet dreams, for instance, when you wake up to find that you've just come, are caused by a build-up of millions of sperm that don't care whether you have any plans for them or not. They just have to get out.

The sperm are catapulted out of your penis with tremendous force, enough to propel them well up inside the vagina, and well on the way to the egg of their dreams. They travel suspended in a fluid called semen, and under a microscope they look like a herd of maddened tadpoles.

Whether all their energy is rewarded or not depends on whether there's an egg waiting for them at the end of the vagina. Because unlike sperm, which are always there, the female egg is a much more modest creature who only makes an appearance once a month.

What happens is this. Each month, the female body goes through a process called the menstrual cycle, which normally takes 28 days. On the first day, an egg cell in your ovary begins to grow. Over the next 14 days or so it develops until it's ready to leave the ovary. It then spends several days travelling through the Fallopian tube on the way to the uterus. If

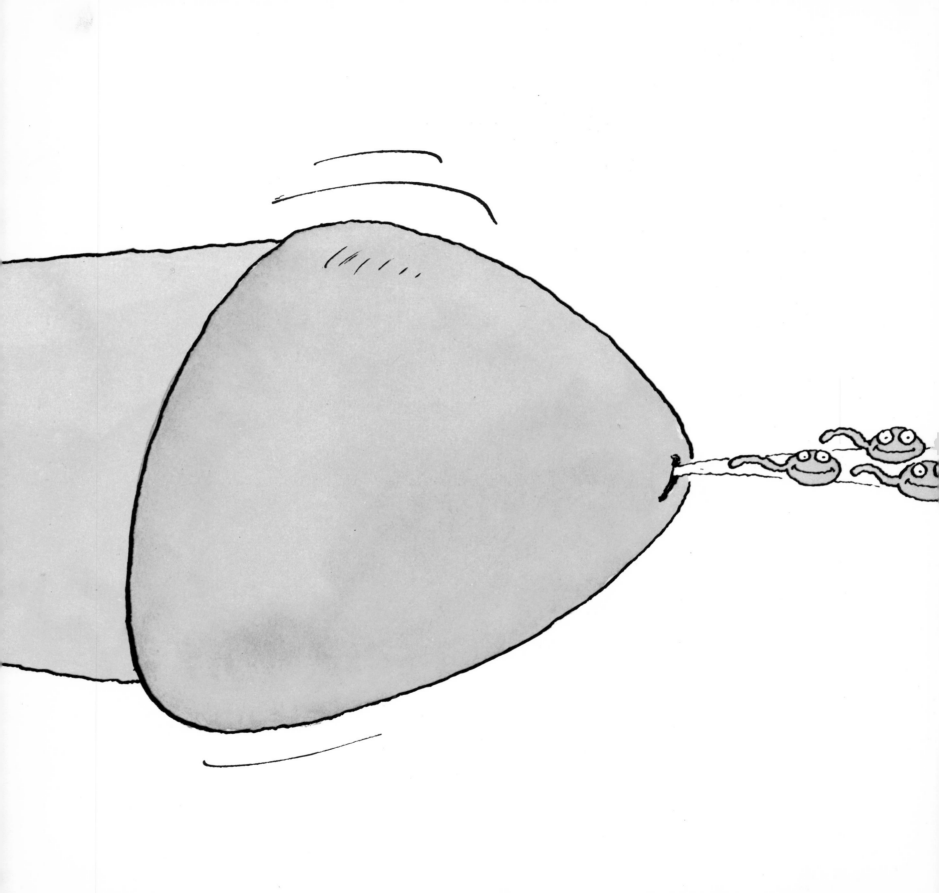

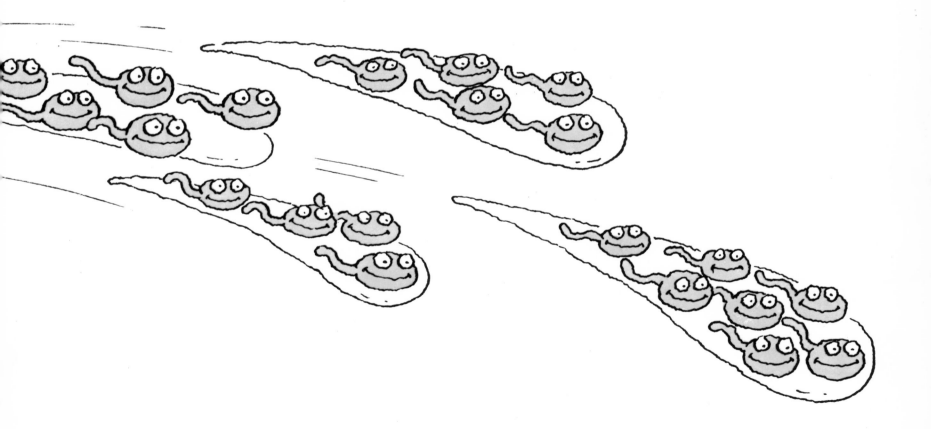

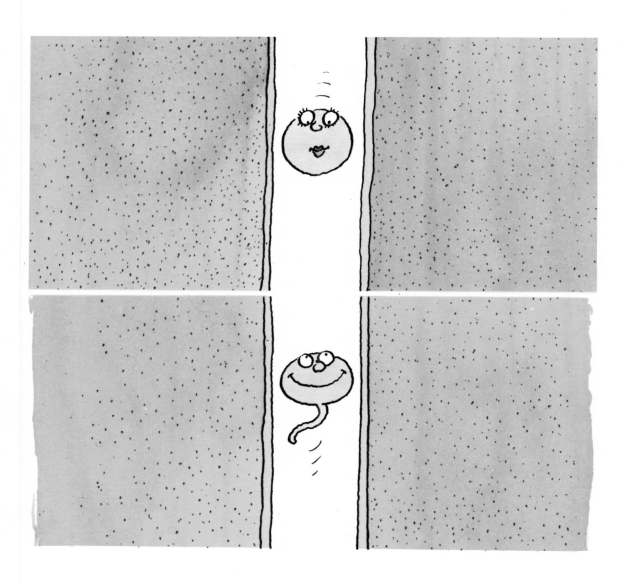

it doesn't meet any sperm on its travels and remains unfertilized, the egg is discharged from your vagina during your monthly period, and then the cycle starts all over again.

So for some of those 28 days (what optimists call the 'safe' period), the egg is tucked away and can't be fertilized. But during those few days spent in the tube, anything can happen. If the sperm rushing up meet the egg coming down, it can be love at first sight, and the next thing you know you're pregnant.

The egg and the sperm combine to form an embryo. And over the next nine months, this gradually grows into a foetus. You can see from the chart what happens during each of the nine months of pregnancy. Let's hope you don't really need to know until you're ready for it.

PREGNANCY BY NUMBERS

ONE
The first month sees the embryo grow from a microscopic dot into a tooth-sized morsel. Even at this early stage, there is a tiny backbone, a beating heart, and the beginnings of arms, legs, nose and eyes.

TWO
Arms and legs are doing nicely, and are joined by fingers, toes, elbows and knees. A definite face is also forming.

THREE
The vocal chords, much used in later life, begin to develop.

FOUR
The foetus is now about the size of your hand, and beginning to get lively. By the end of this month it's usually possible for the mother to feel distinct signs of activity.

FIVE
That embarrassingly bald head sprouts a thin covering of hair, and nails begin to grow on the fingers and toes. The heartbeat is audible, if you have a stethoscope.

SIX
Eyebrows and eyelashes form, and the eyelids open for the first time.

SEVEN
The foetus has now grown to a weight of about three pounds, and the brain is starting to grow too.

EIGHT
Great activity on all fronts. Everything grows furiously.

NINE
A final spurt of growth as the foetus gets ready to make an appearance.

Although this is a book about birth control rather than birth, we thought it was worth including this very brief summary of a pregnancy for one reason: to help you realize how quickly the egg and the sperm turn into a tiny person. A lot of people don't take pregnancy seriously – or don't even believe it's happening – until three or four months have passed. By then, as you've seen, the foetus has become well-established and quite well-formed. After five or six months it's a living human being rather than an abstract idea, and it's too late for you to have any second thoughts.

REDUCE SPEED: OBSTACLE AHEAD

All of us, male and female, are virgins until we've made love. In the case of the man, virginity is nothing more than a label. But with a woman, there's usually a small but important physical difference which separates the virgin from her non-virgin sister. It's called the hymen. The hymen is a thin film of skin which lies in wait for the unsuspecting penis at the entrance to the vagina, making the entrance a lot smaller than it otherwise would be. Not all hymens are alike; some are tougher than others. And not every girl still has a hymen by the time she grows up. It is, after all, just a membrane, and it can get broken by all kinds of activities that don't have anything to do with sex. Horse riding, bike riding, gymnastics – they've all accounted for their share of broken hymens. So you can see that it's not by any means an immovable object. (Having said that, it's only fair to add that there is the occasional very tough hymen which needs to be enlarged by a doctor. This isn't difficult. He can do it right there in his office, and we're told it hurts about as little as having your ears pierced.)

Let's assume that your hymen has survived the rigours of horsebacks, bicycle saddles and parallel bars, and that it's still more or less intact. What do you do about it when you want to make love?

As you've just read, the entrance to the vagina is partly closed. There is an opening, but often it's only large enough for a finger to get through, so a penis is going to find it a very tight fit. Fear not. The hymen, like the vagina itself, is elastic and can be stretched. You can do it yourself – first with one finger, then two, then three; or your partner can do it for you. Gradually, the hymen will stretch until the entrance to your vagina is large enough to allow the penis in.

But don't rush at it. Even after all your stretching exercises, it will still be a tight fit. You may find that the hymen will tear slightly as the penis goes in, and there might be a few drops of blood. But providing you take it easy, and providing the man behind the penis is gentle, you'll be too busy to feel any more than a momentary discomfort.

OPTIMISM: THE WORLD'S WORST CONTRACEPTIVE

You've probably heard the story that nature gives all virgins a free trial run. In other words, you can't become pregnant the first time you make love. Sad to say, this is nonsense. Sperm and egg cells don't know the meaning of beginner's luck, and if you make love at the appropriate time during the menstrual cycle, pregnancy can happen just as it can with a couple who have been making love for years.

It's not even necessary for the penis to make a complete trip up the vagina. Sperm are resourceful and determined little creatures, and they can travel what for them are enormous distances under their own steam. Once at the entrance to the vagina, their instinct is to press onward and upward, with or without the penis, so be warned.

In the next chapter, you'll find a complete guide to all the popular forms of contraception. Some of them aren't much use to girls who have hymens, as they involve a device that has to be placed at the top of the vagina. But there are two kinds of contraceptive that are particularly good for first-time users: the pill for women, and the condom for men. Without going into all the details here, it's worth mentioning them just to emphasize

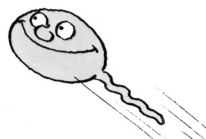

the importance of using something other than optimism at the start of your sex life.

SEX FOR BEGINNERS

The first time you make love is one of the very few occasions that you remember for the rest of your life. Whether it's a pleasant memory or something you'd love to forget depends to a certain extent on luck, but much more on the amount of thought and preparation you put into making the great moment a success.

After years of youthful anticipation, your natural reaction is probably to go at your partner with all the finesse of a dieter attacking a chocolate cake. If both of you feel like that, fair enough. More often, though, one or both of you will have first night nerves, and trying to hurry things along is likely to end in disappointment, frustration, and three of the most deflating words in the English language: "Was that *it?*"

With something as personal as making love, it's

impossible to suggest a plan of action that will suit everybody. But here are some general hints which we hope will help you decide who you make love with, and where and when.

THE RIGHT PERSON

The best definition we know of the right partner is someone you'd like to wake up with. If you're not quite sure, ask yourself a few questions: for example do you *like* each other? (A very different feeling from physical attraction or infatuation.) Do you have anything in common besides sex? Are you kind to each other? Would you go on spending time together if for some reason you couldn't make love? Can you talk to each other honestly about sex?

The more no's you answer, the more you should think again. It would put an impossible burden on your sex life if that had to compensate for an otherwise empty relationship.

THE RIGHT TIME

This has nothing to do with clock time. Sex can be good (or bad) no matter when you have it.

What we're talking about is *enough* time. A hurried half hour is no way to start your sex life, for two reasons. First, a time limit is enough to make you nervous even if you weren't already. And more important, when you restrict the available time you inevitably restrict the enjoyment as well. If making love were a simple mechanical matter of penis and vagina getting together, a few brisk minutes might be enough. But sex can and should be a lot more than that. Just in practical terms, most women need and enjoy a certain amount of stimulation before the vagina is ready for the penis. And the half hour or so of total relaxation immediately after orgasm is one of the great luxuries of life.

So don't skimp on time. Allow yourselves three or four hours at least. The bedroom is no place for a stopwatch.

THE RIGHT PLACE

The right place is somewhere you can both relax, and this will obviously vary from couple to couple. There are some fearless souls who can, and apparently do, manage very nicely behind a bush in the park, in the back of a plane, or in the front of a car. It's not always because they can't find anywhere else; the risk of discovery actually adds to their enjoyment. But for most of us, sex is private, and even the thought of a gallery of spectators is quite likely to bring the proceedings to a full stop. Making love while looking over your shoulder is not one of the more popular positions.

Apart from anything else, it's uncomfortable, and discomfort can turn your moment of passion into an obstacle course. If you're too cold, too cramped, or too worried about the neighbours popping in, you're giving yourselves an unfair disadvantage. If your bodies are constantly being prodded by rocks in the ground, or those knobs that mysteriously grow all over the inside of a car, it's hard to ignore them.

As a good general rule, if you wouldn't be reasonably comfortable sleeping on it, don't try making love on it. Not the first time, anyway.

HOPEFUL, MECHANICAL AND CHEMICAL

The basic types of birth control.

The theory of birth control is simple. All you have to do is prevent the sperm and the egg from getting together.

But as you've gathered by now, it's not quite as straightforward as that. Mistakes can happen all the time, and they do—caused by lack of knowledge, forgetfulness, not reading the instructions on the back of the box, or just plain bad luck. Part of the medical profession spends the best years of its life searching for the foolproof and totally comfortable contraceptive that you take once a year and then forget about, but it hasn't happened yet. Until that happy day, we must make do with what there is.

We've divided the range of options into three sections, and given each method of contraception points out of ten on a combined comfort and reliability basis. Some are better for one partner than for the other, which is why the points awarded by the vagina often don't agree with those given by her friend. But since you'll probably experiment with two or three different forms of contraceptive before you find one you're both happy with, you'll soon work out your own scores. Our rating system, incidentally, is not based on any kind of medical or scientific analysis—just practice. We'll start with the least satisfactory.

HOPEFUL

Coitus Interruptus is the scientific name given to the most unscientific and primitive method of contraception that there is. People have been trying it for years without causing even the smallest dent in world population growth.

What's supposed to happen is that the man withdraws his penis from the vagina just before coming, and thereby stops his sperm from meeting her egg. The odds are almost as bad as playing Russian roulette with a machine gun, and you would have to be desperate to attempt it.

The major physical snag is that sperm have no idea of neatness and order, and they don't all wait in tidy ranks until the moment of ejaculation. A small advance party can leak out of the penis long before the others, and they can cause conception just as easily as their millions of friends waiting behind.

Apart from that, the mental and emotional disadvantages are enormous. The strain on a man's self-control is often unbearable, the worry on the woman's side is impossible to ignore, and the resulting tension is enough to kill any real chance of sexual enjoyment. Add to that the feelings of frustration, guilt, and lack of fulfilment on both sides, and there you have coitus interruptus. If you think you'd have more fun going to the movies, you might just be right.

The Rhythm Method gets its name not, as you might expect, from some musical infertility rite, but from the rhythm of the model 28-day female menstrual cycle.

We've already been through the cycle, so you know that for several days before the start of your period, and again for several days after it has started, you're supposed to be able to make love without conceiving. (The 'safe' period.) It's those few days in between you've got to watch. (The 'sorry' period.) To make things more complicated, the cycle doesn't always stay the same. It can vary from month to month, depending on your emotional or physical condition.

The main problem with the rhythm method is that it's not by any means precise, and therefore not at all reliable. To have any confidence in it, you need a menstrual cycle that functions like clockwork despite illness, travel, emotional ups and downs or anything else that could throw the timing off by a crucial day or two. And how can you be sure of that?

There are, it's true, ways of working out your safe days. The least complicated involves taking your temperature each morning and marking it on a chart. (You can get a special chart from a family planning clinic or a doctor.) You'll find that your temperature drops slightly when the eggs are being produced, and then goes up immediately afterwards. Once this higher level has been maintained for at least three days, it's usually fairly safe to make love. However, don't bet on it. To quote the population expert, Dr. Paul Ehrlich, "People who use the rhythm method are commonly called parents."

The one advantage of the rhythm method is that it is the only form of birth control approved by the Catholic Church. If that affects you, get yourself a chart and a thermometer. If it doesn't, you'd be better off with one of the other methods.

The Vaginal Douche is unromantic and unreliable, but it's better than nothing. You need a vaginal syringe or a special douching bag, and the idea is to wash away the sperm in the vagina before there's any chance of conception. As it's impossible to be sure that water alone will do the trick, most douches on the market contain a chemical sperm-killer. That in itself can be a reason for not using a douche: the chemicals may irritate the walls of your vagina. But worse is to come. While the douche may or may not kill the sperm, it will certainly put an end to any romantic thoughts of lingering in bed with your loved one.

Since the effectiveness of douching depends on catching the sperm before the sperm catch the egg, speed is of the essence. You have to be out of bed and sprinting for the bathroom as soon as possible after orgasm, instead of enjoying that relaxing half-hour with your partner. Not the best way to end an evening.

MECHANICAL

The Condom, or sheath, has been with us for hundreds of years. In the days of Casanova, condoms made of sheep gut and tied with a ribbon were popular with young men about town. Today, rubber has taken over, the ribbons have disappeared, and a whole range of more streamlined models is available.

You can get condoms in different thicknesses and different colours, and with exotic additions like fringes, bumps and ticklers, but the principle remains the same. You roll the condom right down from the tip to the base of the penis; a small sac at the business end catches the sperm and prevents them from reaching the egg.

There are a couple of possible disadvantages. You may find that the mechanical act of putting on the condom interferes with your lovemaking. On the other hand, if you both join in, the process of rolling it on can add to the anticipation of what comes next.

The other minor disadvantage is that a condom will obviously lessen those delightful sensations felt by the penis. But what you lose in sensitivity (and it's not much), you gain in the length of time you can hold on before coming.

As a general rule, the thinner a condom is, the more it costs. And the more decorative it is, the less reliable it's likely to be. Even less reliable are the cheap unbranded versions, so stay away from them.

On the whole, though, we are great fans of the condom. It's relatively cheap, very easy, highly reliable (the people who work these things out say it's 96 per cent effective), and you know it's there. The loss of sensitivity is slight, and the peace of mind for both of you is a tremendous encouragement to relax and enjoy yourselves.

Hints for the first-time user.

1. Make sure you put on the condom *before* the penis has had any contact with the vagina. One drop of moisture on the end of an erect penis can carry thousands of sperm.

2. Trim your fingernails, and make sure you don't leave any jagged edges which may tear the rubber.

3. Be careful, when you and the condom make your exit, that

you don't spill the contents anywhere near the vagina.

4. Don't be stingy. Use a new one *every time*.

5. For belt and suspenders enthusiasts, you can use a spermicidal jelly as well — just in case any sperm escape.

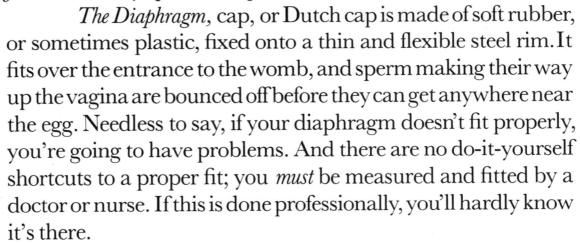

The Diaphragm, cap, or Dutch cap is made of soft rubber, or sometimes plastic, fixed onto a thin and flexible steel rim. It fits over the entrance to the womb, and sperm making their way up the vagina are bounced off before they can get anywhere near the egg. Needless to say, if your diaphragm doesn't fit properly, you're going to have problems. And there are no do-it-yourself shortcuts to a proper fit; you *must* be measured and fitted by a doctor or nurse. If this is done professionally, you'll hardly know it's there.

When you go for your fitting, you'll usually be given a practice diaphragm to try out for a week or so before you graduate to the real thing. This is not intended to be a reliable contraceptive. It's to help you get used to putting the diaphragm in correctly. Because, unlike the IUD, which is worn all the time, you only wear a diaphragm when you're making love. That doesn't mean to say you have to leave it until the last minute; you can pop it in hours beforehand. In fact, it's much better to do it when you're not in a tearing hurry to get to bed, because you're less likely to make a mistake. A nearly accurate fit isn't good enough.

As a second line of defence, your doctor will probably suggest that you put spermicidal cream or jelly along the sides of your diaphragm before you use it. With this, and a professionally fitted diaphragm, you can relax. The two combined are almost as reliable as the pill.

Here are one or two tips for the beginner:

Don't remove the diaphragm for at least six hours after making love. You can keep it in for longer – up to 24 hours if necessary. After that, you should take it out and wash it.

Use a mild solution of soap and water. Detergents and strong soaps can damage the rubber.

So can sharp fingernails. It only takes a tiny nick to make even the best-fitting diaphragm less than reliable. Those sperm get everywhere.

Go back to the doctor or clinic every six months for a check-up. Your diaphragm may have stretched.

IUD is the common abbreviation for the inter-uterine device, which is fitted into the womb. It can be made of plastic, nylon, stainless steel or copper, and it comes in a variety of shapes: loop, coil, 7 or T.

First, the good news. The IUD is extremely reliable – about 98% effective. It's also very convenient. Once the doctor has fitted it (and it must be fitted by a doctor), there it stays. You can forget about it except for a check-up once or twice a year.

Funnily enough, not even doctors are certain quite how the IUD works. Whether it causes the female body to produce a substance that neutralizes sperm, or whether it prevents the fertilized egg from implanting itself in the womb nobody knows for sure. What they do know is that it works.

And now for the bad news. If you happen to be one of the unlucky minority, the IUD can have serious side-effects. It has been known to cause peritonitis, blood clots, cramps, urinary infections or growth of facial hair. It can become displaced, or even fall out completely.

But these alarming cases are very rare. You can be reassured by the fact that millions of women around the world find the IUD comfortable, reliable and trouble-free.

CHEMICAL

Spermicides act like a contraceptive safety net. Used on their own, they don't provide enough protection to rely on. But they can sometimes come to the rescue if your condom springs a leak or your diaphragm isn't fitting as snugly as it should.

Spermicides kill sperm. They're inserted, in one form or another, into the vagina before making love. (Not, as some dissatisfied customers have done, afterwards.) You can take your pick from any of the following forms.

• Suppositories look like elongated tablets. Using your finger, you push the suppository up to the top of your vagina a few minutes before making love. Your body heat then dissolves the suppository and the spermicide spreads around. Don't keep suppositories in your pocket; they melt easily.

• C-film is a small sheet of film impregnated with spermicide which dissolves inside the vagina. Again, you can use your finger, or place the film over the top of the penis.

• Foams, creams and jellies are squirted up the vagina with the help of a plastic applicator rather like a syringe.

• Foaming tablets about the size of a well-known headache remedy (which, in a way, they are) are slightly quicker and easier to use than other forms of spermicide, but there's not much in it.

You'll find a range of spermicides at most good druggists. Experiment until you find the form that suits you best, but don't count on them for reliable protection. Always use something else as well.

The Pill is generally reckoned to be the most reliable form of female contraceptive. The reason for this is the way it works: instead of attempting the risky business of trying to prevent the sperm from meeting the egg, the pill either inhibits or prevents ovulation completely. If ovulation doesn't take place, there's no egg. If there's no egg, there's no baby.

All you need to contribute is some simple bodily mathematics. You take your first pill on the fifth day after the start of a period, and then one pill a day for 20 consecutive days. You then stop. One to three days after that, your next period should begin. On the fifth day, you start taking the pill again.

After a couple of months, it becomes as automatic a habit as cleaning your teeth.

The advantages of the pill are obvious. It's almost totally reliable. It doesn't interfere with lovemaking. You don't feel it, your partner doesn't feel it, you don't have to stop to take it, and a month's supply takes up less room than a bar of chocolate.

The disadvantages are the side-effects that sometimes occur, ranging from a gain in weight and feelings of biliousness to depression, high blood pressure and thrombosis.

We're not trying to put you off. There are, after all, more than 50 million satisfied pill-takers throughout the world. But what you must remember is that the pill causes changes in your body, and it's not something you fool around with. You must get your doctor's advice before starting, and if your first brand doesn't agree with you, go back for a change of prescription. There are plenty of different formulations, and unless you're very unlucky you'll find one that suits you.

The Ultimate Contraceptive

Every year, more and more men are having a simple, quick operation called vasectomy. It's done with a local anaesthetic, it doesn't require a stay in hospital, and it is a completely reliable method of contraception which doesn't affect your sexual drive at all.

All that happens is that the tubes which carry sperm from the testicles to the penis are snipped and closed off.

That's it. No sperm – no babies. Ever. And there's the only problem. The result of a vasectomy is permanent. You can't change your mind a few years later and therefore you can't ever have children of your own. Which is why most men wait until they have children before they have a vasectomy.

A NASTY BUT NECESSARY GUIDE

People don't like to talk about venereal disease. It's an area of sexual knowledge which is still surrounded by guilt, fear, silence and ignorance – a combination that guarantees the continuing rise in VD statistics. (They're already incredibly high: for example, there are about 16,000,000 reported cases of gonorrhea throughout the world each year. That's just the official score for just one variety of VD. If you include unreported cases, and all forms of sexually transmitted diseases, you'd probably have to double that figure.)

If VD were considered more of an ailment, and less of a sin, it would be easier to admit to, easier to treat, and perhaps possible to get rid of altogether. Since that isn't likely to happen, you'd better know about it.

The first piece of news we ever received about VD was a solemn warning that you caught it from sitting on a toilet seat. Filled with dread, we spent several uncomfortable and often constipated years before finding out the truth: the way you catch VD is through sexual contact with someone who already has it.

The best and most simple form of prevention is knowing your partner well enough to be sure that he or she isn't infected. Unfortunately, even that isn't foolproof, as you'll see later on, so you should have a basic knowledge of the symptoms to watch out for. Here, starting with the worst one of all, are the most common forms of VD.

Syphilis.

Syphilis can kill. Henry VIII died from it. So did the Emperor Nero. And despite modern antibiotics, about 20 per cent of the people who catch syphilis today may eventually die because of it.

The first sign of syphilis is a red spot which appears at the point where the germ entered the body – usually the genitals, but sometimes the mouth or rectum. This can happen at any time from ten to ninety days after infection. The spot turns into a hard sore, and is followed a few weeks afterwards by a more general skin rash. At this stage, syphilis is highly infectious.

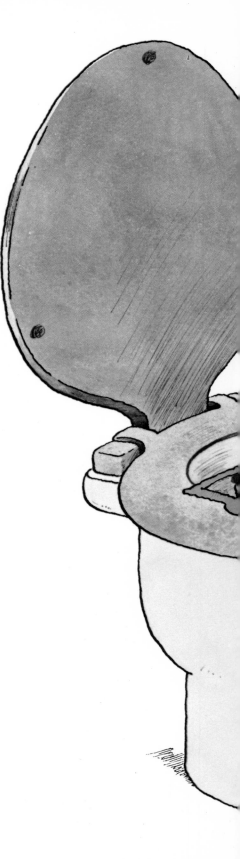

During stage two the symptoms disappear, even without treatment, because of the natural defences set up in the body. If you're lucky (and the odds are not good), these home-grown defences will cure the disease completely.

If you're unlucky, the symptoms will disappear but the disease won't. It may stay inactive for many years, but then stage three will develop, often with horrifying results such as brain damage, blindness or heart disease. It doesn't even stop there. An unborn child can inherit syphilis from the mother.

The cure is a course of injections of penicillin and other antibiotics. But it must be taken early, and under medical supervision. So if you think there's any chance you've caught syphilis, see a doctor *at once*. Treated early enough, syphilis can be cured quickly and completely. But it's important to remember that the course of treatments must be completed and checked before you can heave a sigh of relief.

Gonorrhea.

Gonorrhea has been called 'mankind's greatest pestilence', and the numbers are there to prove it. America alone accounts for more than 3,000,000 cases a year. It's a much less serious form of VD than syphilis, but very infectious and sometimes difficult to detect in women.

The symptoms in the man usually develop within a week or so of infection, with a discharge of pus from the penis and a burning sensation when urinating. Female symptoms are similar—a discharge from the vagina and painful urination—but they're slower to appear and often too slight to be noticeable. A girl could easily have gonorrhea and pass it on without knowing anything about it.

Thank heavens for penicillin. When prescribed in the right dosage, it has an almost 100 per cent record of clearing up the disease. There is some evidence of a form of super-gonorrhea which is resistant to penicillin, but luckily it's not immune to other antibiotics.

As with syphilis, immediate treatment is essential. Run, don't walk, to your doctor or local VD clinic.

NSU (Non-specific urethritis).

Almost entirely a male problem, NSU is like a mild version of gonorrhea. The symptoms are similar but less pronounced: some discomfort when urinating, and a certain amount of discharge from the penis. For once, penicillin doesn't work, but another antibiotic, tetracycline, usually does.

TV (Trichomonal vaginitis).

To even things up, TV is almost entirely a female problem (in fact, it can sometimes cause NSU in a man). Symptoms are vaginal discharge, and soreness and itching between the thighs. But relief is just a few swallows away — medically prescribed drugs will sort you out in no time.

Honeymoon bladder.

This is often the result of too much of a good thing. Enthusiastic and prolonged lovemaking can shake up the female bladder and cause the owner to urinate much more frequently than usual. If there is any pain or bleeding, see a doctor. But don't worry about it. A few days rest will have everything back to normal.

Crabs.

Pubic or crab lice like to make their home in the hair round the genitals, and can spread from there right up to your eyebrows. You catch them (or they catch you) as a result of contact with an infected partner. Cure is by powder, spray, lotion or shampoo containing a lice-killing ingredient. Prevention is much easier; crabs hate soap and water, and won't nest in clean surroundings.

Other disorders.

There are some other rare problems that may affect the genitals, such as tiny warts. If you notice anything unusual, see a doctor. Normally, there's nothing much to worry about, but it's good to have a professional opinion.

Prevention and cure.

We live in perilous times. The combination of increased sexual opportunity and a reluctance to get proper treatment has made VD more common than measles used to be. You probably know someone who has it.

There's no way you can be sure of never catching VD unless you're prepared to keep away from sex altogether. However, there are some basic precautions you can take. They don't provide complete insurance, but they help.

First, know your partner. Since you know each other well enough to go to bed together, you might think this is unnecessary advice. But most cases of gonorrhea are caught from friends who aren't friendly enough to be honest about their problem, or who aren't really sure they have one. That applies to you too. So if either of you has any doubts about your genital state of health, head for the doctor instead of the bedroom.

Using a condom helps, too. Apart from its valiant service as a contraceptive, it will also give you some protection against VD, although it's not the great cure-all some people believe it to be.

Finally, use the bathroom. Urinating after making love and washing thoroughly with soap and water are both good habits to get into. If there's a bidet handy, use that. If not, you can always make do with basin, bath or douche. Or better still, take a shower together.

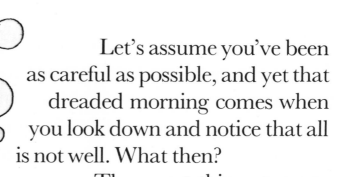

Let's assume you've been as careful as possible, and yet that dreaded morning comes when you look down and notice that all is not well. What then?

The worst thing you can do is keep quiet and hope that it will go away. The chances are that it won't. And in the case of syphilis, ignoring the signs could have serious and long-lasting effects on you and maybe your children as well.

Unfortunately, there's no private and easy way out. If you think you've caught VD – any kind of VD – you must get medical treatment. Refusing to have it properly treated is anti-social and potentially dangerous. Self-treatment is unreliable at the best of times, and some of the do-it-yourself remedies are positively harmful. There's no substitute for qualified medical attention.

Your regular doctor is the best person to see, and immediately is the best time to go. The sooner VD is treated, the sooner it's cured. You needn't feel you're a special case; most doctors have treated dozens of VD victims. But if you can't face the thought of going along to the family doctor (who is often a family friend), call your local Health Department for information about special VD clinics. They may not be the most pleasant places, but at least nobody knows you, and treatment is completely confidential.

While you're being treated, avoid having sex. Otherwise you'll just be adding some other poor soul to the statistics. And try not to feel you've committed some terrible crime. VD is only dangerous when you don't get it treated.
Catching it is just rotten luck.